PENGUIN

LIVING THINGS

PENGUIN

Rebecca Stefoff

BENCHMARK BOOKS

MARSHALL CAVENDISH
NEW YORK

Benchmark Books
Marshall Cavendish Corporation
99 White Plains Road
Tarrytown, New York 10591-9001

Illustrations by Turi MacCombie

Library of Congress Cataloging-in-Publication Data
Stefoff, Rebecca, date.
Crab / by Rebecca Stefoff.
p.   cm. — (Living things)
Includes index.
Summary: Examines the physical characteristics, life cycle,
and natural habitat of different species of penguins.
ISBN 0-7614-0446-5 (lib. bdg.)
1 Penguins—Juvenile literature. [1. Penguins.]
I.Title. II. Series: Stefoff, Rebecca, date.   Living things.
QL696.S473S72 1998   597.47—dc21   97-8940 CIP AC

Photo research by Ellen Barrett Dudley

Cover photo: *Peter Arnold, Inc.*, T. Thomas

The photographs in this book are used by permission and through the courtesy of:
Peter Arnold, Inc.: Bios/Thierry Thomas, 2, 19; Allan Morgan, 8; Roland Seitre, 8-9,
13, 16-17, 18, 22; Kevin Schafer, 10; Doug Cheeseman, 20 (bottom); Fred
Bruemmer, 21; Gunter Ziesler, 32. *Animals Animals*: Johnny Johnson, 6-7, 7, 9, 17,
24, 25, 27; Doug Allan, 12; Fritz Prenzel, 23; Ben Osborne, 26. *The National
Audubon Society Collection/Photo Researchers, Inc.*: Tim Davis, 11 (left and
right); Rennee Lynn, 13 (inset); Rod Planck, 14; Joyce Photographics, 15; Suen-o
Lindblad, 20 (top left); George Holton, 20 (top right); Noble Proctor, 20 (bottom).

Printed in the United States of America

1 3 5 6 4 2

For Katherine Grace Vibbert

king penguins, South Georgia Island

emperor penguins, Antarctica

The far southern part of the world is a land of rock and ice and snow. Here is where penguins live.

Each year thousands of penguins meet at nesting grounds called rookeries. Soon the mother penguins are bringing their babies into the world.

Penguin mothers and fathers take turns on the nest, protecting their babies. And they take turns feeding fish to the hungry young chicks. The chicks need to eat a lot. They grow very fast.

Penguins help each other with chick care. One grown-up penguin babysits many chicks while their parents go fishing.

emperor penguins, Antarctica

A chick grows and grows until it is almost as big as its parents. It is covered with thick, soft, furry feathers. Emperor penguin chicks are gray, with black-and-white heads. King penguin chicks are brown.

One day the chick starts pecking at its feathers. It pecks and pecks until all the fluffy chick feathers come off. Underneath is the penguin's grown-up suit: a smooth, shiny coat of black and white feathers.

king penguins, South Georgia Island   *king penguin*

After a penguin sheds its chick feathers, it sets out on its own.

Penguins are birds, but they don't fly. Instead, they use their short, stubby wings to balance themselves as they waddle along.

Adélie penguins returning to rookery, Antarctica

Adélie penguins

When penguins want to go fast over snow, they flop onto their stomachs and push themselves forward by digging in with their feet. On slippery snow a penguin can slide downhill on its stomach—just like you slide on a sled.

Adélie penguins

Adélie penguins

No one teaches a young penguin how to swim. It just walks to the edge of the ocean and knows what to do.

Penguins swim very fast and very well—almost like flying in the water. They spend hours in the icy water every day, feeding on fish or small sea creatures called krill.

Adélie penguins

king penguins with fur seal, elephant seal

Seals cruise these waters, too. They are looking for penguins to eat. At the slightest hint of danger, the penguins pop out of the water.

On land, seals aren't such a threat. These two seals are in a fighting mood, but the king penguins easily stay out of reach.

Adélie penguins, Antarctica

emperor penguins, Antarctica

Antarctica is the coldest land on earth. When winter comes, many penguins leave for islands where it is a little warmer. But the emperor penguins stay. They are the only animals that spend the winter on the Antarctic ice. They even lay their eggs there, holding them on their feet to keep them off the cold ground.

royal penguins, Macquarie Island

yellow-eyed penguin, New Zealand

Magellanic penguin, Falkland Islands

Galápagos penguin

jackass penguin and cormorant, South Africa

Not all penguins live in ice and snow. Some kinds of penguins live on grassy islands. Others live on the coasts of South Africa and South America. But all of them live in the southern half of the world.

A few kinds of penguins have feathers that stick out or up from their heads. This is the rockhopper penguin. It lives on hilly islands and gets around by hopping from rock to rock.

rockhopper penguin, Amsterdam Islands

little blue, or fairy, penguins, Australia

The little blue penguin is the smallest penguin in the world. It's only fourteen inches long (36 centimeters)— smaller than these two pages put together.

king penguins, South Georgia Island

When a male king penguin is ready to mate, he walks up and down making loud calls. This is called trumpeting. A trumpet is a kind of horn, and the penguin's calls sound like a horn blowing.

When penguins mate, they stay together for the rest of their lives. Penguins may look alike to us, but each one can pick its mate out of a crowd of thousands.

king penguin trumpeting

gentoo penguin with egg, South Georgia Island

For weeks the penguins guard their precious eggs and keep them warm. Then the eggs hatch, and the rookery is loud with the squawks of baby penguins. New life is beginning in the lands around the South Pole.

gentoo penguin with chick

A QUICK LOOK AT THE PENGUIN

Penguins have been around for a long, long time. Fossils show that many kinds of penguins lived on the earth 50 million years ago. Some were bigger than today's biggest penguins. Most of these ancient penguins disappeared long ago. Today there are only seventeen different kinds of penguins in the world. None of them lives north of the equator.

Here are six kinds of penguins, along with their scientific names and a few key facts.

LITTLE BLUE, OR FAIRY, PENGUIN

Eudyptula minor
(yew DIP tew luh MY nor)
World's smallest penguin. Stands 14 inches tall (35.5 cm) and weighs 2 pounds (0.9 kg). Lives in southern Australia and in the nearby island nation of New Zealand.

ADÉLIE PENGUIN

Pygoscelis adeliae
(pie go SEH lis ah DEE lee yay)
One of most common penguins in Antarctica. Also the penguin most often seen in zoos around the world.

GALÁPAGOS PENGUIN

Spheniscus mendiculus
(sfeh NIS cus men DIH kew lus)
World's rarest penguin. Lives near
the equator, on the Galápagos
Islands. Currents of cold water from
the south polar region allow it to live
in a warm climate.

KING PENGUIN

Aptenodytes patagonica
(ap teh noh DYE teez pa tah GOH nih kuh)
Second-largest penguin. Stands 40 inches tall (1 m) and
weighs 40 to 60 pounds (18–27 kg). Lives on the coasts
of Antarctica. Females nest twice in three years, laying
one egg each time.

ROCKHOPPER PENGUIN

Eudyptes chrysocome
(yew DIP teez cry so KO meh)
Stands 25 inches tall (63.5 cm). One of several
species of crested penguins. Lives and nests on
steep, rocky islands near Antarctica. Climbs by
hopping, using flippers for balance.

EMPEROR PENGUIN

Aptenodytes forsteri
(ap teh noh DYE teez FOR steh ree)
World's largest penguin. Stands about
48 inches (1.2 m) tall and weighs 55
to 70 pounds (24.75–31.5 kg). Lives
only in Antarctica. May walk 50
miles (80.5 km) or farther from
coast to nest.

Taking Care of the Penguin

In earlier years, penguins were hunted by humans for their meat, skins, and
oil. Today most countries have agreed to protect penguins from hunting.
And in order to keep penguins with us for everyone to enjoy in the future,
we must be careful not to spill oil into their waters or to disturb the small
islands where many of them breed.

Find Out More

Arnold, Caroline. *Penguin.* New York: Morrow Junior Books, 1988.

Coldrey, Jennifer. *Penguins.* London: Deutsch, 1983.

Johnson, Sylvia A. *Penguins.* Minneapolis: Lerner Publications, 1981.

Lepthien, Emilie. *Penguins.* Chicago: Childrens Press, 1983.

Paladino, Catherine. *Pomona: The Birth of a Penguin.* New York: Franklin Watts, 1991.

Strange, Ian. *Penguin World.* New York: Dodd, Mead, 1981.

Tenaza, Richard P. *Penguins.* New York: Franklin Watts, 1980.

Index

Rebecca Stefoff has published many books for young readers. Science and environmental issues are among her favorite subjects. She lives in Oregon and enjoys observing the natural world while hiking, camping, and scuba diving.

Magellanic penguins, Patagonia